THE JOURNEY
OF LIVING

Self Discovery

With,
Blue Bear Encounters!

B. Louise Bayer

BALBOA.
PRESS
A DIVISION OF HAY HOUSE

Balboa Press books may be ordered through booksellers or by contacting:

Balboa Press
A Division of Hay House
1663 Liberty Drive
Bloomington, IN 47403
www.balboapress.com
1 (877) 407-4847

Print information available on the last page.

ISBN: 978-1-9822-0523-2 (sc)
ISBN: 978-1-9822-0524-9 (e)

Balboa Press rev. date: 12/12/2018

Blue Bear

We need answers to our questions!
Where do we go?
Blue Bear has patience, and,
Blueberries galore!

With Blue Bear observations...
Come evaluations!

Asking for delivering...
In believing, to receiving,
Looking around...
Where can Blue Bear be found?

Like the wind...
We can feel Him,
With the sun and the moon...
Blue Bear is more than a whim!

Having, to knowing, to feeling...
The Encounter meeting,
There's magic in believing!

CONTENTS

Preface

While reading over my book, "Thoughts for a Lifetime" feeling somehow, there must be continuations. But continuations of what? Maybe, "Thoughts" can be condensed even further...into verses? Those angels were trying to tell me something. Perhaps more playful and fun.

Feeling under angel control, and with the Blue Bear energy ready to feed me with insight into what I had already written; and what I was contemplating on writing.

So, for you, this is how the verses came about. I had never written a poem in my life. How could this possibly happen? Asking for help, equals a commitment made. A door opens! Going inside one's self-realization, is the reward. There's a lot of good stuff in there. True magic!

Now, what have I done? There's no turning this energy off. To do something I have never done before, where do I start? My thoughts seemed to be all jumbled up. Maybe our bookstore will have some ideas. Indeed they did! A rhyming dictionary. But after a while, like the dictionary, I hardly used it. It became a tool of sorts.

Putting "Thoughts" into rhyming verses was a challenge, but so much more, and fun. To arrange negative thoughts into a positive way of thinking, in cadence, came to be the result. The process was so inspiring; thoughts started coming out of me like a race horse running.

And now, my introspective reader, you can read some of the creations for yourself. With your own notebook to record your own thoughts, let the journey begin. From inspiration to activation, comes your own creation!

SEARCHING

CONTENTS

Our Pathway to Follow

With a blind horse...
Pulling our wag-gon,
Reins in hands...
We drag-gon!

Searching and believing...
With a wagon to fill,
Trusting in the unknown...
Just over the hill!

From a map of inspiration...
Moving along a trail,
With a sign painted...

"Lives under Construction"
We wail!

Actually, John Madden was my inspiration for these verses. During a football game he used this description, "A blind horse pulling a wagon." Wow! That comment spoke volumes to me. There are times when we need to be brave and trust. But, it's very important to do our homework, and being prepared, is the name of the game, for the best end result!

Our Relationship to the Earth
"Airtos"
(As it relates to our soul!)

Placing our feet on the ground...
Breathing in the atmosphere,
Survival could begin here...
With nothing to fear!

From the sounds of the earth...
Surrounding us,
With invitation...
Like linking up a chain,
For a celebration!

Wherever we go, wherever we are...
Whatever we do,
We are feeling our worth...
As we are connected,
To the earth!

Above us, beneath us, and...
To the moving water,
Our chain becoming ever stronger...
Celebrating the living earth,
The generous earth...the active earth!

With the power of light,
The secret of night...
Waking us up,
To over-coming our plight!
All...
As it relates to our soul!

"AIRTOS!"

All through the writing of "Thoughts" my little word "airtos" kept me grounded, and focused as to keeping it all honest, truthful and real. "Airtos!"

What Comes First...
Changing or Growing?

Changing for growing, like the seasons...
There are reasons!
The seasons teach us about changing...
For re-arranging,
Winter is for recovery...
While spring, is for discovery,
Summer, is about sun-bathing...
Fall, shows us colors blazing,
All the while, we're growing...
Without realizing,
We're transforming!

We're moving, for improving,
Rendezvousing, reviewing, then...
Pursuing,
Our lives are changing...
All the while,
We're growing!

Most of us are reluctant to change anything, for whatever reason. Why is that? Because, changes bring on alterations? Blue Bear says, "Flexibility for adaptability." In order to advance, one needs to be open to what that change might mean, or offer. It could mean fruit in the summer, pumpkins in the fall, winter snow for skiing, and spring flowers for baskets hanging. All requiring some kind of motivation for activation, for growing.

Courage...and, Where We Find It!

Courage isn't something...
We automatically know,
It's like having an automatic pilot...
Set to go!

Courage comes along...
With our miscellaneous, and being...
Spontaneous!

It's like having our own sponsor, director, and producer,
Doing what comes naturally, voluntarily...
With spontaneity!

Courage is something very near...
If we're looking for courage, we'll find it,
Facing the unknown...
Without fear!

I believe I was watching TV when someone said, "That took a lot of courage". All of a sudden that angel/blue bear energy kicked in.

Imaginings to Experience

From the oak tree, comes the acorn...
Through our imagination,
Ideas are born...
Then,
Capturing the determination, of...
A Capricorn!

Do we build a picket-fence?
Or,
Consider the evidence?

Ideas are blooming...
With mounting suspense,

We're building a pathway...
To our experience!

This must have come from thinking about "the follow-thru concept" with anticipation of the out-come.

Our Imagination

Our imagination is a wonderful tool...
For thought,
A tool that cannot, by any means...
Be bought!

Our imagination becoming an anchor, for...
Centering our attention,
Using our imagination, for...
Bringing our emotions,
Into the equation!

Blending heart, mind, and spirit...
Fulfilling our imagination...for,
Making an imaginary tool, of...
Our own creation!

It's about going full circle, but knowing and understanding what that full circle amounts to. A soul searching process...mind, body, and spirit.

Influencing Ourselves

Our involvement in life has meaning, but...
What part are we playing?
Contributing in ways,
That may not be revealing, but...
There's magic in believing!

Having our mental swords, for...
Yielding benefits, and rewards...with,
No holds barred!

Influencing ourselves, with...
Our imaginary,
Elves!

It's about getting the job done from the resources we've created! And, it was about this time that I began feeling that there was something more than my angels helping me; besides you and me, there is this other energy.

Living Life Full-ly

Life doesn't come...
With money back guarantees,
Going after what we want...
Being on time,
Or, with no absentees!

Giving a commitment, of...
Our best energies,
With no certainty, for...
Deliveries!

Patience and willingness, to...
Live life...full-ly,
Reaping the benefits, however...
Un-rule-ly!

What I think I'm trying to say here is: "Nobody is going to do your job for you". Once done, don't expect any acknowledgment. The completion is in itself, the reward.

Reaping What We Sow
One faces the future, with one's past!

To reap what we sow, can be...
A negative way of thinking,
Making one stop to think:
"What am I creating?"

Past and present...
Rolled into one,
Give some ideas, of...
Lessons, to come!

Responses today, give-way, to...
Experiences, from yesterday,
Whose roots lie deep in the past...
Preparing a means...to,
Create a new cast!

Requesting a play...
Destined to be remembered,
Lessons learned...
While going thru life,
Dis-membered!
What talent there is...
Will be put to the test,
The attraction will be handled...
Predicting a new,
Fore-cast!

Reaping what we sow...
Can be, a good thing,
You know!

Being fearless, living in gratitude, having faith in one's self. Rewards
abound!

What Would We Come Up with, For...Describing Ourselves?

We'd like to think, "We're as solid as a rock!"
But, inside that rock...
There's something we're concealing,
With a pad-lock!

What could be so revealing?
Could it be, that inside, we feel all coiled up...
Like bed-springs?
Feeling like a truck, bent up with dings...
Needing a fixing up...with,
Some con-fide-ings!

Holding it together, means...
Creating a façade,
All buff, shiny, and clean...
Prancing down an arcade,
Ready for the parade!

Who are we fooling?
What happened, to...
Our schooling?
Freeing ourselves from guilt,
With, our home-made quilt!

By going back to our past, for...
Some visitations...
Acceptance of...our,
Imperfections!

Facing up to ourselves is sometimes...
A hard pill, for us to swallow,
Respecting ourselves...
Is what follows!

Let's just say, for...
Describing ourselves:
"We're not afraid...
To make, the marmalade!"

Going thru the process, from fear and doubt, to being truthful, to being prepared, to self-honesty, to over-coming, to acknowledging, to self-respect, to empowering...for being ready for life! "Well done!" You might want to create your own list and process of prioritizing! It's a Blue Bear thinking thing!

Our Everyday Lives

Personal experience has taught us, to...
Center ourselves,
In the face of demands,
Smoothing our passage, for...
Other commands!

There's a grand scheme to trust, and...
A rightness that beckons,
Leading us on...
With a force, that reckons!

Our knowledge derives...
From our everyday lives,
Becoming, our archives!

Accomplishments, with our over-comings, becoming our epitaph!

Is Re-Direction What We Need, Or...What We Want?

Our deeds travel with us, from afar...
And, what we have been,
Are what we are!
George Eliot

Change can only come...
From within us,
Starting with re-direction...
And deep searching...
Alongside of honesty,
And trusting!

This act of re-direction...
Can be painful,
Mind, body, and spirit...
Going thru the process is suffering,
And distressful!

Wanting or needing...
Takes a lot...of,
Re-thinking and re-directing...
About painful changing!
Now!
Needing or wanting...
More opportunities, for expanding,
And developing...
Our inner-growing!

Being open for self-honesty, acknowledging growing can be painful, but rewarding.

Loving Ourselves First Then...Others!

When harsh words are spoken,
To what equivalent...
Self-love requires conditioning,
And a shell, as a repellant!

Our outer behavior matches...
Our inner state of mind,
While understanding and forgiveness...
Are there, for us to find!

Knowing that love comes, from...
That special place within,
Loving ourselves first...
And others,
Then!

Understanding where we're coming from in our relationship to others.
Where are you coming from?

Daring to Try!

Facing the challenge of...
Discovering one's talent!

Do we accept the invitation, or do we relent?
We want to find out, what is pertinent!

Do we bake a cake, or go find the rake?
We could get our fishing gear, and...
Head for the lake!

Our interests are confusing, and varied...
Finding the right transportation,
To be carried!
Catching the right boat...
To be ferried,
We're searching for, our destination,
And, not to be hurried!

Our curiosity leads us to many doors...
Defying fear...we go inside,
To explore...
Exposing what lies hidden!
We're here to acquire,
To get over, the quagmire...
To fix, the flat-tire,
To walk, the high-wire...
Face the building on fire!

We may cry...
But,
We're daring to try!

Being tenacious with determination...whatever it takes.

Assuming

We have a tendency to make assumptions,
Due to our inter conflicts, or...
Having the courage to ask the questions!
Being impeccable with our communication...
What fear could there be in asking...for,
Clarification?

Wiping the slate clean,
Creating a clear vision, for...
Understanding a difficult situation,
Amplifying an agreement, for discussion...
Being realistic about,
Making a foolish assumption!

Assuming can be consuming...
Much better for us to be,
Un-assuming!
With ears ready for receiving,
Whatever the heart, may be feeling!

Where people are concerned, assuming is not where we want to go.

REACHING

CONTENTS

Coaching

Training to teaching...
Learning the game,
Expanding one's thinking...
The coach's job is motivating!
Building a structure, from...
Instructions to, executions...from,
Exhilarations...to exhaustions...
On to recommendations...from,
Expendable to commendable, to...
Dependable!

The coaching continues...becoming a team,
Moving forward...gaining some steam!
Coaching, or playing the game,
In sports, or in life...
The name's the same!

Singing an anthem as an epitome...
Guarding the encroaching,
Applauding our coaching!

Understanding, it takes a strong foundation for self-coaching. More foundation building coming, as we move along. Also, becoming a good, or a better listener.

Prophets and Poets

It's to our human condition...
That prophets and poets are speaking,
With a challenge, or consoling!
A less complicated way of seeing,
Tearing away a veil, for revealing...
Understanding, with inspiring words,
And singing!

Prophecy or poetry, is having the ability,
To see thru, complex machinery!
Explaining every day events...
In a language, with components,
That suit the moments!

Making running verses...like marching to a cadence,
Writing verses, with circumstance, and...
Singing with exuberance!
Prophets and poets...
Igniting and delighting...with,
Imaginative and inventive...
In-sighting!

Thinking before doing!

Acknowledging Life...
As a Phenomenon

Not knowing which words we utter...
Might be words of wisdom to another!

Considering Shakespeare as a pioneer...
For lighting the chandelier,
Appreciating the veneer...
For a new kind of premier,
Taking a time-out for a croissant...
With a glass of Sauvignon Blanc,
Not fully cognizant, of our confidant!

Placing an ad in the classified, for...
Becoming a guide, to provide,
Going on a hay-ride...
Feeling like Jekyll & Hyde,
Preparing to collide!

We're off, with possessions to pawn...
Looking for our icon,
We'll log on, for tickets to Milan...
Then, off to the Parthenon!
We'll visit The Hanging Gardens of Babylon,
We'll add on The Amazon...
Do a walk on in Oregon,

Acknowledging life as a phenomenon,
We have a lifetime of feelings and emotions...
That count!
Worthy of Paramount!

Life is full of surprises and opportunities, along with identities!

Pass the Lemons, Please!

Oranges are good for us, but...
Lemons make us think!
By drinking lots of lemonade...
We might avoid the shrink!

When life goes rinky-dink...
Lemons, keep us in-synch,
Having a time-out, with a cool...
Lemonade drink!

We need our lemon zest, for...
Feeling our best...for,
Creating a manifest, for...
Taking a trip to Budapest...for,
Solving problems of, common interest!

We have a request!
Please come to America...
To be our house guest!
We'll have a meeting on, East meets West...
Speaking of concerns, for...
What's on our chest!
We're ready for our lemons, to...
Start the process,
But first, we'll take a recess, to...
Play a game of chess!

No need to second guess...
We're here to relieve the stress,
Cancel the anti-freeze...
Pass the lemons, please!

We'll consult with Hercules...
Then off, to the Florida Keys,
Where we'll enjoy the white sand beach...

The palm trees, and the cool breeze...so,
Pass the lemons please...
Along with the cheese!

We'll reminisce, doing "The Twist"...
We'll enlist The Swiss,
For keeping time.
They never miss!

We'll get to the bottom of this...
Then, seal it with a kiss!
Forget the exorcist...
Lemons exist,
Not to be dis-missed, so...
On with the contest!

"Geese" Louise,
"Pass the lemons...please!
We're ready for the trapeze!"

Life is about being prepared, no matter what we have to go thru!

23

What Value We Give,
To...Collecting Things

Eyes light up to things of attraction,
Creating a feeling, of...
Much satisfaction,
Collecting and keeping...
Fulfilling a need,
An anchor and identity!

Without our collection...
Where would we be?
In flotation...
Without our personality!

By going inside ourselves we'll find...
Treasures of another kind,
There's value galore...
Inside our store,
Finding the shelves ready, for...
Collecting more!

Acknowledging just what we are collecting...tangible and intangible?

A Vision for Ourselves

Acknowledging our own empowerment...
Is to grasp,
The fleeting moment!

We have the potential...
To chart our own course...or,
We can choose to stay stuck...
In yesterday's remorse,

Following our vision...
To capture...
Our identification,

A powerful preparation...
For the actual trip,
To our destination!

How do we become a real person? Could it be by keeping it real, keeping it honest, keeping it truthful, always actual; according to our own actuality? And, what is your actuality? By now, no doubt, you're feeling a bunch of stuff, to think about.

Alterations, to...Confirmations!

Going for the chase...
To win the race,
With pounds added...
Changing the application,
For entering the race!

Having a hand with 4 aces,
Encouraging us...
To pick up our paces,
Taking another look...
Our aces becoming erases...with,
A royal flush, changing the look...
On our faces!

Hitting the ball foul...
Going back to our bases,
Reconsidering our chances...
For, re-adjusting our places,

From alterations...
Come calibrations,
For making, recommendations...
From translations,
Come confirmations!

On to receiving praises...
Along with,
Well-deserved raises!

Effort equals our reward!

Secrets!

Secrets, when locked away...
Become secrets that can cause decay!

When does something under wraps...
Make us want to run some laps?
Then to,
Take some naps, to...
Wake up...to find,
Some traps!

Revealing what's on our shelves,
For becoming...
Our better selves!

A broken-wing bird cannot fly...
To our secrets,
We say:
"Good Bye!"

Self-truth comes first, freeing us to live our life fully. Without truth and honesty, where would our integrity be? It wouldn't be!

Consciousness of Thought

The power of the mind,
Equals the awareness, of...
Our consciousness,
Gifting us with a present, for...
Our thoughtfulness!

Somewhere in our consciousness...
Lie the answers to our questions,
Allowing us to recognize...
In the form...of,
Our expressions!

Awareness of our consciousness...
Guiding and directing us,
Thru bewilderment and despairing...
On to understanding...and,
To our forgiving!

Going beyond our intellectual analysis,
To our consciousness, the catalyst...
Consciousness of thought,
Is caught!

Thru understanding, forgiveness becomes possible!

What Disturbs Us, Can Be Confusing!

"We learn silence, from the talkative...
Tolerance, from the intolerant,
And kindness, from the unkind"
Kahlil Gibran

Should we be grateful to these teachers...for,
Living life more fully?
By creating a relativity, thru negativity...for,
Forming our positivity?
It could be time for us, to take a consensus!
We're learning more about ourselves,
Thru what, is disturbing to us!

Valuable in-sights for lighting up our senses...
For, taking down our fences,
Serving to amuse us...
And, to unconfused us!
Lessons deserving of our attention...
Having created a nuance...of,
A revelation!

From negativity comes our positivity

Words Taken Personally

When thoughtless words are spoken...
It's easy to be offended,
Offering an opportunity for deleting, or...
Re-phrasing,
Then on, to be amended!

Taking a stand, in one's defense...
To question one's find-dings...for,
Favorable new bind-dings!

Maintaining an image, of...
Self-respect, takes courage,
Refusing to take anything personally!
Instead, hand and hand,
Giving love...
Un-conditionally!

A self-gifting gift: Giving love unconditionally!

FINDING

CONTENTS

Finding Security

Are we just a part of a data base...
That one computer could erase?
Where is our anchor, and...
Where is our base?

For some it's religion, for others,
Politics is the race!
We crave security, but...
Where is our certainty?

Feeling like a pioneer, we volunteer...
All in good cheer!
No need to go for Sherlock,
We have our bed-rock!

What we have is found from within...
With our anchor,
Securely hooked in!

Always our bedrock is knowing one's self: Being sincere, truthful, and honest.

The Dependable Heart
In a word: Devotion!

Our ever beating heart,
Began its journey early on...
With a rhythm as constant,
As a pendulum swinging...
In a protective cage,
With flesh clinging!

Life's blood surging...
Through a network of vessels,
Supporting a human...
On a mission, with muscles!
When muscles grow weary...
The tireless heart,
Goes right on thump-ping...
Maintaining a system,
Without ever think-king!

Our heart would be a great teacher, but...
That's not its job,
Just doing its business...
With nary a sob!

This was my 2nd set of verses. It was Valentine's Day. Otherwise, it's
a mystery to me where these verses came from; inside my thinking.
An interesting phenomenon...a Blue Bear thing, I think.

The Journey that Matters!

To our lives...
Our goals lend direction...
Providing substance...for,
Our self-definition!

With a task well done...
Comes a feeling...of,
Much satisfaction!

Developing the process,
Passing thru...
The myriad of activities...and,
Unexpected barriers...
Following the highway...to,
Un-suspected carriers!

Traveling the by-ways, the sky-ways...
And onto our drive-ways,
A journey with purpose...
Delivering us home,
With a surplus!

We've created a fort-tress, with...
Limit-less rich-ness,
Arriving at our destination, to...
Discover, it is endless!

Discovering purpose! Passing it forward! Always, with continuations!

Action over Depression

Be it a mild disgruntlement...or,
Serious frustration,
Concern should drive us into action...
Not, into depression...or,
Couches with cushions!

Offering emotional support to another...
May be all that is needed,
Following thru, with a prayer...
Not, to be defeated!

Reality of emotions and feelings...
Intangibles, not to be seen...but,
As tangible...
As an on-coming train...or,
A jelly-bean!

Wow! Facing whatever may have been the realities of life...for me, at
the time.

Descending to Ascending
Power of the mind

Experiencing emptiness...
Bewilderment...and,
Des-par-ring...
Is the lack of love... and,
Understanding!

Looking inside...
Beyond our intellectual elements...to,
Determine our nature, for...
Future developments!

Purity of thought re-gaining,
Turning into feelings of love, and...
Comprehending!
Consciousness of awareness...
Expressions of thought,
Are sought!
Ideas unfolding into thinking...
Through that,
Our realities are caught!
From our depths, to our heights...
Going inside to visualize,
Ready for us, to...
Realize...

The power of the mind...
Is there for us to find,
Empowering ourselves, from...
Descending, to ascending...
On to amending...and,
Revealing!

Acknowledging the dilemma...to over-coming the negative feelings,
whatever they may be; and on to: realization, to activation, for
satisfaction!

Our Moving Pathway...
Are We On-board?

Moving along our pathway...
It's up to us...to,
Discover our course,
We're moving forward, for...
Finding our source!

We're moving in a direction...
But, where is our destination?
We'll give a deposition,
To acquire...
An acquisition,

Guiding our ship into port...
Arriving with our passport,
But feeling...
A need to abort!

There's a blue-jay...
Showing us a gate-way...for,
Writing our screen-play...
"Going Thru Life, in Disarray!"

Celebrating our pathway-essay...
Having found our cachet,
Toasting with a glass, of...
Pouilly-Fuisse!

Following the pathway...
Across the causeway...to,
Thunder Bay...
Having found,
Our forte!

Acknowledging one's place in the world.

To Love One-another

To love one-another...
Is a moment to capture and treasure,
To let grow into habit...
Becoming one's own second nature,
To love...
Is to place our happiness...
In the happiness of another!
With,
Selflessness, comes broadening our vision...
Beyond self-serving needs,
Fostering positive feelings...
Creating good deeds!

Our personal happiness grows...
When,
We nourish someone else's...
Delivering an abundance of,
Elevated pulses!

So true!

Free to Love

Setting those we love free...
To love us in return,
We may need to take a U-turn...
Go on a sojourn!

We'll eat crocodile tail fricassee,
Served by Dundee!
Then off...
To the Grand Prix jamboree!

Enjoying drinking Long Island ice-tea...
Feeling fancy free, with no guarantees!
To return...
We'll need a trustee,
With a pass key...
To face the committee!

Having learned the evidence of love is...
Commitment to another's development,
Helping another to discover...
Their own special gifts,
Delivering to us...
Our own special lifts!
Free to become...
Our own special ones,
Living our lives...
In unison!

Developing selflessness!

Nature of the Journey,
Past, Present, and Future...
Being One in the Now!

Embracing our past, respecting our history...
Facing the future, needn't be a mystery!
Past and future being joined...
By the present,
Becoming our "Now", and...
Our equivalent!
Living with our "Now"...
Containing much alarm-mo-ny,
Creating a rapport...
Uniting with our harm-mo-ny!
Living in the "Now" is a new way of being...
Giving us, a new-born way of feeling!

Being one who has arrived,
At a new destination...
In defiance of gravity,
Receiving an un-familiar, levitation!

Seems like we tend to think about tomorrow, while living in our
"Now". Why is that?

The Brain verses the Mind

The "brain" and the "mind"...
Are not the same!
"Biological" is the brain's claim,
While "Spiritual"...
Is the mind's game!
To learn the "facts"...
The brain goes to college,
A duality emerges when the mind...
Gains the knowledge!

The brain is all knowing,
Then, the mind comes along...
With...
Education showing!
A purpose with intentions...
Ready for conventions!
There is no end, or limitations...
Or,
Boundaries,
For this relationship's...
Synchronizations!
Knowing the facts...
Doing what matters,
The brain, with the mind...
Avoiding disasters!

The brain verses the mind. This was Blue Bear's idea, giving us
something else to think about.

Doing Our Best

Having opportunities, or...
Over-coming obstacles,
Facing the unknown, and...
The unforeseen,
Whatever the cause...
Always doing our best,
Without wavering, or...
Taking a pause!

When put to the test...
It's our job to do,
Our very best!

Action to satisfaction...
Filling our treasure-chest!
Doing our best...
To conquer our quest!
Being and doing...
Always,
Our very best!

How we show up, being prepared, and willing to do whatever the task may be.

Hoping verses Wanting...

What are we wanting, and...
What are we hoping?
Is hoping, the "consideration"...
While wanting, the "operation?"
Hoping without action...
Leads to little satisfaction!

During difficult times of coping...
"Where are we with our hoping?"

Making progress...
Moving toward success!
Our hoping with our wanting...
Believing in delivering!
Encouraging and supporting...
Stating and reporting,
Succeeding with blending...
Our hoping, with our wanting!

It's all effort producing, with a commitment in the making!

Our Thought

With the divine tool of thought...
Being our own teacher,
Is caught!
Having an instrument...
That cannot be bought!
Gaining a mind of virtue...
Is sought!

Thought, is a created agent...
Showing us life,
Guiding us from start to finish...
Through our strife!
In the course of...
Our thoughtful thinking!
With the master key...
To our reality,
The door opens...
To our capability!

Something to think about! Do we really realize how much we have to think about, and are capable of doing. Excavation to/for realization!

From the Blueberry Patch

Blue Bear has...
  Blue Bear language!
    With muscles for helping...
      Not threating!

With a voice...
  for caring,
    and a love,
      For sharing!

An Introduction

It was Valentine's Day, and I had been invited to dinner. A little gift would be nice to take. Among my collection, there was something I thought would be just right. The only card I found didn't have a verse inside. "What will I write?" The Every Ready Bunny came to mind. Only, I would make it, "The Every Ready Angels!" Something short and sweet would be good. It went like this:

The Ever Ready Angels

Our soul-full hearts...
With soul-full darts,
To flow into...
Our soul-full parts!

Our homes contain un-conditional love,
Where only soul-full food is served...
And soul-full music is heard!

Our mission is soul-searching...
For soul-full-lu-tions!
A full-time job,
With angels singing...
To love one-another,
With arms, ever reaching!

These were my very first verses! And, an unbelievable breakthrough! I had no idea what was in store for me...I had never written rhyming verses before!

Well, when I returned home than evening, there was more: "The Dependable Heart!" (Page 36)

The verses just took off from there. And, I had felt for some time, that there was this energy I could count on for answers. Then, I thought I had to give it a name! The feeling was strong and male-like. Since I am, B. Louise Bayer, why not, Blue Bear? That was it, my "go-to guy" became, "Blue Bear".

When I had completed, "Thoughts for a Lifetime" I began thinking, "Isn't there more? There's always more!" For whatever reason, going back over "the chains", (where much had already been condensed) I felt that, "Thoughts" could be condensed even further. From somewhere, the verses came to mind. I'm already writing metaphorically! Why not in verse? And, I have this helper!

At our bookstore, I found a rhyming dictionary. It did come in handy, but after a while, it only became a tool; the verses started appearing before me.

And now, here they are for you; introducing you to: "The Blue Bear Energy!" "What! I'm more than that!" See what I mean? He's a more than helpful fellow!

Given in love,

B. Louise Bayer,
(aka) Louise Martens
louise.martens@att.net
(307) 899-0608

Locating the Blue Bear

Blue Bear is somewhere, but where? There must be some kind of special place. But what do we have to go on? Locating Blue Bear is important!

Are you thinking there is a whole lot of stuff in the way, keeping us from our Blue Bear? Yes, there is! But that's okay! We're just wanting to feel the connection.

From wanting, to believing, to delivering, it will happen! Yes! We've made it to our "Blue Bear" location.

Now, what are we going to do with this discovery? All of a sudden, there "it" is! We have our, "go-to" place! Our answer place! Our warm and cozy place! Our cared about place!

Being with Blue Bear has to be the sweetest, purest, our most un-conditional love place, ever! And, like "courage" if we go looking for Blue Bear, we'll find him!

Let the journey continue!

CONTENTS

Our Tool Chest
Blue Bear Appears!

Quandary or puzzle, and...
Seeing no solution...
Where are the tools...for,
Achieving our resolution?

When put to the test...
Looking into our tool-chest,
Making a request...
An answer comes thru!

"For solving your problems...
There is your mind...but,
Asking your heart,
Would be a great find!"

Little Lou responds:
"So, bring on the sunshine!"
An answer comes through:
"Growing, then showing,
It's all in the knowing!"
We now have the tools...for,
Writing our own constitution, for...
Evolving another revolution!

"What's your name?"
"I'm Blue Bear!"
"Thank you Blue Bear!
So very nice having a friend like you!"
"So, let's go find Celeste,
To see what's in, the bird's nest!"

So, they're buddies! Blue Bear and Little Lou!

Knowledge, with Heart and Spirit

Going beyond our intellect...
Becoming our own architect,
Being lead to our project...
Where heart and spirit are there...for,
Us to collect!
Connecting us to a feeling, of...
Reverence and wonder,
Experiencing lightning, and...
Thunder!
Waking us up, to our heart with our spirit...
We've earned our permit,
Now ready, for the cockpit!
"Greetings!"
"Full knowledge of what changes you...
Is the knowledge you seek!
Having developed your very own...
Phenomenal technique!"
We've got Blue Bear...
In the pilot's seat!
"Thanks Blue Bear!"

Accepting the Blue Bear energy is up to you. I'm feeling: "Why not?"

Is It Co-operation, or...Separation?

Close your eyes...
And don't be afraid,
We're going on...
A crusade!

Being one with another...
Holding paws,
Coming together, for...
Showing a cause!

It's a meaningful operation...
For feeling, a connection,
But, where is our destination?

We're activating...
Our blueberry education!

Blue Bear is here, with his cheer:
"So much more fun sharing a shore...
I know where there are,
Blueberries galore!"

Well, open your eyes, and...
You will see blue,
The fuzzy Blue Bear...
Smiling at you!

So much more fun...
With co-operation, instead of,
Separation!

Are you with me?

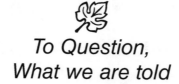

To Question,
What we are told

As a child,
We saw the world flat...
As a door-mat!
That we'd have to go around the world,
To see a wombat!

How confusing, perplexing, and...
Down-right baffling!

Blue Bear is here...
For, dis-entangling,
With some, in-vesti-gating!

Blue Bear sees a clear view, for Little Lou:
"When the sun...
Is out of sight for us,
On the other side of the world...
Its daylight,
Now, hug me tight, and say...
Goodnight!"
Finding out for ourselves, to...
Question what we are told,
We may need to take a poll!

Climbing the scaffold...
We're on the threshold...of,
Discovering our latitude...
Along with our longitude...for,
Achieving...
Our magnitude!

"Goodnight Blue!"

Blue Bear is true blue.

When the Student is ready,
The Teacher will appear!

Along with some shifting...
We're ready for some up-lifting!

Will it take a teacher, or an engineer?
To show us how to use,
Our metaphoric gears?

Deciding on Paris, to...
Become a financier...or,
Going to Venice, to...
Become a gondolier?

Having our own wheel, and...
Not knowing where to steer!

For, mountaineering,
There are the Grand Tetons...
The Lion's Club...for,
Volunteering!

With no deviation...
We want to adhere,
Looking for our cheer, with...
A Samuel Adams beer!

This is the year, with...
The right atmosphere,
Moving in a direction, for...
A meaningful career!

With Blue Bear, the teacher, and...
The student sincere...when,
The student is ready...
The teacher will appear!

You'll see! It will happen!

Unlocking Our Potential...but,
Where is the key?

Developing our talents, is the task at hand!
Do we pick up a baton, and...
Wave a command...or,
Do we take a trip, to...
Our heartland?

Rounding up cattle...
Near The Rio Grande...or,
Follow Alice, into wonderland?
We're for making better choices,
Than Custer's last stand!

There's no acquisition, without application,
We'll need a manifestation!
Compliance with continuous effort, and perseverance...
Will assure us of, goal completion!
Our inspiration becoming...
Our motivation...
Moving on to activation,
With the key, in the ignition!
"Hitting the ball off the tee...
Seeing your name on the marquis,
Driving in the Grand Prix!

You've achieved,
Your Blue Bear degree!"

"Congratulations!"

Walking the Talking

What has to happen, for us...
To walk the talk?
Where is our command, for...
Making the demand?

How do we put into practice...
What we know and understand?
We need a game plan!

Watching Tom Brady could be revealing...
Along with Peyton Manning!
But, for advice...
We'll go Blue Bearing!

With Blue Bear explaining:
"Saying what you're meaning, and...
Meaning what you're saying,
Then doing!"

That's Blue Bear's way of caring and sharing,
Blue Bear is good at simplifying!
Talking, with no fear and doubt,
When...
We go walking about,
We're walking the talking!

Yes!

Can What Is Un-see-able...
Be Believable?

Our feelings are un-deniable...
From sources, always available!

Physically, we are touching...
Emotionally, we are vocalizing!
What else is un-see-able,
But, believable?

Rain is...evaporate-able,
Wind is...blow-able,
Air is...breathe-able,
Sunshine...makes life live-able!

From our unseen sources...
Come forces!

Sounds, with hear-ability...
Energy, with feel-ability...
Leading us to...our,
Do-ability!
All un-see-able,
But, believe-able,

It's, Blue Bear-able!

Intangible to believable!

Finding our Awareness

For finding our awareness,
Where does one look?
Does "it" come from a book?

Asking our five senses...
What would be the consensus?

Our surface tells us hot from cold,
With our eyes, we can behold,
With our ears, sounds unfold!
Tasting can be good or bad...
While smelling can be a warning,
For alarming, or...
For blueberry muffins in the oven!
Would you have a serving?

Blue Bear is true to Little Lou:
"Awareness comes from friendly faces, and...
When you say your graces!
Awareness comes from filling your spaces, and...
Taking your places,
Even, running the bases...
Putting roses in vases...and,
Going those extra paces!
By going inside...
You'll find your mind...for,
Revealing an awareness, of...
Another kind!"

"Blue Bear, you are my Valentine!"

Indeed!

63

Blue Bear is always listening!
Are we listening back?

Looking for that door, to...
Our inner workings,
That certain door labeled:
"Mindful think-kings!"

Hearings words from...
Another source,
Feeling a connection...
To a mighty force!

With Blue Bear...
Trips are always around the corner,
Helping us to find...
Our place of honor!

Do we take Amtrak, or...
Go for the back-pack?
We may want a Kodak...
For playback!

We'll need our cracker-jacks,
Being prepared...
Is a matter of fact!

Looking out for, the diamond-backs...
Paying attention to, our Zodiac,
All the while, smelling the lilacs!

We're feeling an impact...
Collecting artifacts,
Filling our almanac...
We're developing wings,
Ready for the tarmac!

We're vacuumed packed...
Ready to inner-act,
Traveling with Blue Bear...
There's always feed-back!
He's listening, and...
We're listening back!

Yes! Yes we are!

Our Heredity

Where we land is just by chance!
More like, happenstance!
Accepting our heredity...
Believing in our authenticity,
Agreeing with the Almighty!
Avoiding negativity,
By boosting, our positivity!
We're here,
So, where is our liaison?

We'll hold a telethon...
Run a marathon...to,
The Grand Tetons...
Then, on to Tucson,
We'll call The Pentagon!
With Blue Bear leading the orison:
"For everything, there is a season,
For everyone, there is a reason!"
We can't choose our heredity, but...
We can choose,
Our Bear-a-bility!

"Thanks Blue!

Flexibility for Adaptability

Having flexibility, is a necessity...
For our mobility!
Flowing into our...
Adaptability!
Some say, "It's a matter of growing"...
Then, on to showing!
We're on a track,
But, we don't know where...
We're going!
Requiring some thinking, for...
Developing gears...for,
Some shifting!

Being equipped...
For this kind of trip...
May take some scanning,
For our planning!

We've done our preparation...
For finding our grip,
Now, feeling hip...
Blue Bear says, "Yip!"
"Give it a high-five paw,
Let's make it a law!"

Flexibility, for adaptability!

Yes! And, Yay!

Wanting!

To identify our "wants!"...
Would be, an accomplishment,
For sure, a difficult assignment!

Fear, might play a part!

It might take some excavation, to,
Find the location, for...
Identification!
We need to know, our...
Personification!

Do we look up a tree, or...
Behind our knee?
How do we solve...
This mystery?

Taking a trip of sorts, to...
Make some reports...for,
Creating a plan, so...
We can expand!

Going on an adventure...
Traveling thru our nature!
Taking a ride, for...
Exposing our inside...for,
A trip of this kind...
Has to do with our mind!

With Blue, as our guide director...
No need for a brain doctor!

"Finding your wanting,
Is there, for your harvesting...
But, it might mean some shifting!"

Our motivation becoming our activation, with Blue Bear's attention.
What's your evaluation?

What Would We See... Over the Levee?

Having a cup of tea...
Balancing on our knee,
Celebrating with glee...
Having found the key,
Hanging in the tree...
Growing, on top of The Levee!

Came a Blue Bear warning:
"Look out for the bees!"

Are we ready for having the key?
Once secured, the key contains...
Responsibilities!
Opening the door, for us to enter...
Exposing us, to our center!
We may need a mentor!

Blue Bear's friend, wise Winston Owl,
Has hoo-ty howls, and...
Feathery jowls,
His lecturing and teaching...
Showing us and screeching,
Motivating us, for...
Reaching,
Taking the key, to see...
What's, over the Levee!

With "fear and doubt" in its place, life becomes an adventure!

The Candle and the Mirror!

From the mirror, comes reflection!
Creating energy...for,
Candle ignition!

Trusting the sources receiving...
From motivation to activation...for,
Exploration!

Receiving a measure of enjoyment, from...
Encouragement!

Blue Bear with Yellow Toad...
Reflecting together teaching,
Co-ordination causation, with...
Co-operation!

Using the mirror, with...
Candle application,
They're off...
To the Appalachian!

From unknown sources, come resources!

Agony verses Snoring!

Why is it, that agony...
Sets us spinning,
While contentment...
Creates snoring?
Why it is, that pain is the teacher,
While planting flowers...
Is the feature?
Negativity activates our thinking,
While positivity...
Motivates our sleeping!
Finding our cadence, for...
A meaningful performance...from,
Negativity to persistence, with...
Positivity giving way...to,
Our attendance!
With our "Blue Bear" way of thinking,
Comes our Blue Bear singing!
"No reason to snore...
I know where there are...
Blueberries galore!"

"Blue Bear, you are our refuge!"

71

The Du-al-ity of Our Being!

The character of, our "Being"...
Is our, "Du-al-ity!"
Our mind with our spirit...
Becoming our reality!

Being optimistic, by knowing the facts,
Appealing to our self, revealing...
Is a quality, that attracts!

The stage is all set...the actors informed,
With our knowledge and spiritual thinking...
We are prepared, and fore-armed!

Our thoughts are the camera...
Our eyes are the lens,
Putting them together...
The picture blends!

Combining our du-al-ity...for,
Capturing our create-tiv-ity, for...
Producing our auth-then-tic-ity!

Blue Bear expresses:
"The production is complete!
Let's go for a treat!"

Little Lou is proud of Blue Bear:
"Blue Bear, you are a great director!
What do you think about Ecuador?"

Blue Bear informs:
"We'll find a Conquistador...
Check out the Condors,
We'll have Blue Lobster-thermador,
With blueberry petit-fours!"

"I'm with you, Blue Bear!"

Our mind with our spirit...
The duality of our being,
Is a much better way...
For our seeing,
Being, and doing!

On to our achieving!

From Imprint to Implant!

During the process of living...
Imprinting takes place!
Is this what I wish to embrace, or...
Will it be a waste?

Hopefully, the good prints...
Are the ones that stick!
But mostly,
We learn from the bad ones!
Is this some kind of trick?

We could create an operation,
From imprinting to implanting,
Permanently fixed, so as not to go...
Ramp-pant-ing!

Finding solutions could mean...
Changing some rules,
Being prepared, for engaging...
In duels!

Seems like this implanting thing is taking...
For that,
There is no faking!

"What do we do Blue Bear?"
"Start building bridges!
More than a process...
It becomes an allowance,
To be open for answers to come, for...
Creating a balance!"

Preparing for growth and the shift...
Writing a song and singing:
"We're here building bridges...

Creating implants...
Preparing ourselves...for,
The lift!"

Caring about what we are being influenced by.

Re-Construction!

Life is full of bumps and bruises...
We go on boats, for healing cruises!

What we need, is a plate of armor...
That's not a dish, that we would savor!

We could call, The Extreme Team,
To make an evaluation!
Do you suppose, they would respond...
To our kind, of situation?

Taking in the whole picture...
There's quite a mixture,
We'll need instructions, for...
Installing the fixture!

It might be more fun...
To put our worries in a sack...and,
Head for the track...
To bet on the horses...to,
Recover our losses!

Blue Bear is reminding us:
"You have five rainbow toads, who...
Know all the roads,
To help, with your loads:
Violet for your toes...
For the show, there's indigo,
Magenta to get set, with...
Gold to get ready...and,
Green to go!"

"Blue, I love your solutions!"

Finding Toleration,
for... Our Preservation!

What does it take, for us to tolerate?
Toleration, could cause a tummy-ache!

Never fear...Blur Bear is here:
"Toleration is a state of mind...
Toleration is there...for,
You to find!"

When things go rinky-dink...
Our toleration, may go down the sink!
"Help Blue Bear!"
"With beauty all around you...
There is the clue...no need to fuss,
Toleration will find you!"

"Thanks Blue!"

You don't have to look far to find your tolerance, along with your gratitude.

Where Does Happiness Come From?

Having Blue Bear, as our exploring consultant...
Guiding us thru, what is important!

Having his "Knows"...
Following what is fragrant,
Regarding present conditions...
Observing what is relevant!

With too much attention, being focused on...
One's self,
Going to the cupboard...
To see, what's on the shelf!

Investigating the condition, of find-dings...
This would be a good place, for dine-ings!

With this meaningful discovery...
Revealing a valuable recovery!
Leading us to a course, for action...
Conducting a means, for making a connection,
Taking notes, then indicating...
Points of, attraction...
Creating a situation, for...
A meaningful manifestation!

We now have a description, for...
Where happiness is found!
Blue Bear will make a presentation, for...
Our destination:

"Showing others that happiness is a by-product...
Of an effort, to make someone else happy,
With kind-heartiness, and...
Thoughtfulness!"

Blue Bear continues, exploring and presenting:
"Think of happiness, as feeding a blossom...
Watching it bloom,
Witness for yourself, where happiness...
Comes from!"

Little Lou is perplexed!
"But Blue Bear,
Do we have to wander thru the showers...
To get to the flowers?"
Blue Bear shakes his head and explains:
"Do yourself a favor, Little Lou,
Go to the farm...
To get out of the storm!"

Little Lou loves Blue Bear so much!
Now she shakes her head...
With a question:
"But Blue Bear,
Couldn't you have told us that...
From the beginning?"

Blue explains, with a question:
"Yes, but would it have had...
The same meaning?"

With so many lessons in life, what would we be like if life was all peaches and cream? Blue Bear gives us something else to think about.

Procrastination!

Why do we procrastinate...
Putting off,
What shouldn't wait?
Having fun with our pre-disposition...
Deferring to a later time,
Naturally occurring...
Throughout civilization!

Giving attention to our creation...
Acknowledging our imperfection,
Searching for, our migration...
To reveal,
Any revelation!

Moving on to our investigation, for...
Exposing our procrastination!

"Blue Bear we need help...
The jury is still out!
What are we to do?
How about a day at the zoo?"

"For you, Little Lou...
Let's go to the zoo...for,
Procrastination...
There is no destination!"

So true!

Is What We Want...really, What We Need?

"Blue Bear, what makes needing...
So different, from wanting?"

Blue Bear is thinking:
"While needing is necessary for surviving...
Wanting can go beyond...becoming self-serving,
Wanting or needing, will be put to the test...
When a commitment is made,
To do, your best!"

There's no denying...
Blue Bear is good at simplifying!

Sounds simple! But is it really?

Taking "It" all in,
For...Dishing "It" All Out!

Knowing what the "IT" is...
Would make us resourceful,
But, needing a hint...
So as, not to be mournful!

To continue, the intent...
Desiring to be sent,
To finding, our "IT!"

Curiosity could be, the "IT" to follow,
With Blue Bear, living in a hollow...
Leading us to a silo,
Discovering, lots of milo!

"Thanks Blue Bear, but...
I'm going to find,
My pillow!"

Finding the "IT" is a very difficult job...
Maybe, it's time to call Bob,
We know that Bob can fix it, but first...
We've got to find "IT!"
Did we ever lose it?
That's it!

With our curiosity, we can create...
Our "IT!"

"Blue Bear I'm so glad...
You thought of that!
I mean, "IT!"

What fun!
Taking "IT" all in...
For dishing, "IT" all out!
That's what, "IT"...
Is all about!

Did we really figure the "it" out?

What If...
We had to manage our own anatomy?

Our anatomy was given to us...
From the beginning,
Automatically functioning...
Without our ever thinking,
How utterly amazing!

If we had to manage, our own anatomy,
What would happen, to the economy?

It's a good thing, and comforting to know...
It's all ago, so on with the show!

With Blue Bear, as my constant consultant,
Companion and friend...
More like, a pretend book-end!

"What?"

Just another aspect of one's personality...
A novel idea, of one's own creativity!
"So, Blue Bear, what about our anatomy?"

"It's Mother Nature's job...
To take care of your anatomy,
I do, "angel-ology!""

"But Blue Bear, what about...
The economy?"

"That's your job-ology!"

"Well done Blue Bear! And, forgive me. You are more than a "book-end!" Feeling your support is more than extra special!"

Doubting is Troubling!

Doubting creates barriers, for...
Our endeavors,

When doubting comes to mind...
Defeat, isn't far behind!
Developing good habits...
Is there for us to find!

Using our abilities...
There is our intelligence,
But sometimes, we may need to go back...
To re-claim, our common-sense!

Thinking of the risk...
Seeing an abyss,

Reflecting on our coaching...
The doubting becomes a smoke-ring!
Doubting is a negative...
Until we analyze it,
Doubting makes us stop...
To think a bit, about it!
How good was our mitt, for...
Catching the ball,
That was just hit?

For Blue Bear,
Doubting is a positive, for...
Getting on the bus,
A very good remedy, for what...
Is troubling us!

Good to go for a time-out!

Living Each Precious Moment,
With Intentions!

Intentions of our choosing...
Resulting in our shaping!

With our intentions...
Becoming our experience,
Effecting our resilience!

The process being:
Unconsciously choosing, then...
Unconsciously evolving...or,
Choosing consciously, then...
Evolving consciously!

Be it, dissolving or resolving, or...
Going for evolving!

Being content with our five senses, or...
Being alive in the universe...with,
Our multi-sensory consensus!

External with internal...
Having all five senses...plus,
Being consciously intelligent!

Extending on beyond the physical world,
Watching the domain of Blue Bear un-furl!

Having multi-sensory...
Our intuitions, hunches...and,
Subtle feelings, are closer at hand...
Recognizing a warm heart,
Beneath a harsh and angry manner, or...
A cold heart...with,
A polished and pleasing banner!

With different currents blowing...
Creativity, healing, and love flowing,
Having a positive and purposeful force...
Our soul is with us...for,
The longevity of our course!
Residing in a dwelling...
Of love and understanding,
Acceptance without judgment...
Being a valuable discovery!
Loving and understanding...
Having no constriction,
Is the soul's conviction!

The purpose of our journey...
Is to find our soul's hiding place!
Our five senses having fallen from grace...
With our multi-sensory system,
Leading us to home-base!

Our soul is just as alive as our breathing,
Waking us up to serving...
With, our believing!

(Blue Bear hits a home-run...
With the bases loaded to the limit!
With the Blue Bear,
There's never a dull moment!)

Aligning our personality, with...
Our soul's activity,
Acknowledging the soul's...
Immortality!

Recognition of time,
Isn't within the soul's understanding...
That could be our big finding!
With no limitations, or conditions,
Following the pathway, to...

Our evolutions!

With lessons to learn, and...
Personality taking its turn,
Has the attention, of...
Our soul's concern!

Evolution of our soul,
Delivering its dole...
Following each characteristic:
1) Emotional
2) Physical
3) Psychological
Becoming the experiences, of our soul!

(All in a bowl – one of many!
Blue Bear jumping from one to another...
Looking for the blueberries...
To go with the honey!)
Searching for healing...
Is the soul's reason for being!
Functioning within our velocity...
Being in-tune with our,
Whole-los-ity!

Living each precious moment, with...
Clarifications...of,
Our intentions!

(Blue Bear is holding a challis...
Toasting with a boasting!
Blue Bear's gone...
Up-hill coasting!)

With the Blue Bear, anything is possible!

Finding the Blueberry Patch

"Enlightenment"

Recognizing, to acknowledging, to contributing...
To, our existence,
For, making a difference...
By creating an enlightened experience,
Lighting a torch for illuminating our porch!

Delivering a document,
Attesting to our commitment...
For, making a difference,
Signifying satisfaction, with gratification...
Brightened by illumination,
Confirming our realization!

"Enlightenment is like a beautiful red rose,
Its fragrance fills the air."

"Is that you, Blue Bear?"
"Enlightenment, is a simple way of thinking...
The mind of Humanity harmonizing,
With love, and understanding!"
There is no match...
For, finding,
The Blueberry Patch!

Of course! And, "Thank you, Blue Bear!"

A Mortality Reflection!

Inside our morality sandwich...
What would we find?
A document all signed?
A reflection with no correction, or...
A revealing for appealing?

For locating our niche...
There's a glitch!
Looking for the switch...
To our, mortality sandwich!

We could go Blue Bearing, for...
Blueberry sharing...or,
We could go for seeking...
The Source,
To be, re-enforced!

Now, asking for direction, for...
Making the selection,
Standing at the entrance...
Wanting to advance...to,
Take a stance!
Asking Blue Bear...
"Do we dare take the chance?"

Blue Bear explains:
"By going to, "The Source"...
Claiming your resilience,
Becoming your experience!"

"YUM"
"Thanks Blue Bear...
For showing us, our equilibrium!"

Going for our mortality...
Finding our, im-mortality,
Becoming, our reality!

A mortality reflection observation!

For whatever it's worth to you...a morality reflection!

The World is Waiting!

While the world is waiting...
We're debating!
Storms continuing, creating...
Our fating!

Turbulence beyond our imaginings, with...
Destruction, devastation...and,
People in explosions!

What kind of plan, is it going to take?
With more than one storm...
There are many storms, at stake!

Each storm has its own people,
Intensifying and destroying...
With no rational,
For what?

People wanting to have a voice, for...
Making a choice,
What is it going to take, to...
Open that gate?
Having and living a life, with...
One's own beliefs...
Without violence or interference...for,
All people in attendance!

To bring this turmoil to a finish,
How can freedom be accomplished?

We have Blue Bear describing:
"By flying planes for freedom,
Dropping leaflets from the sky...
With messages from Moms stating:
"We want to live, not die;

Here's why, we should try!"

Answering questions of how...
These storms can be brought to a conclusion,
With questions, to be answered...
With a resolution!

Hundreds of thousands of papers...
Creating an accumulation...of,
Suggestions, on how to re-build...
A civilization!
The world is waiting, for...
This information...
A formulation of rights...for,
All the People!

Voices to be heard...
Speaking the word... for,
Re-building their lives!

With hands ever reaching, with...
Voices teaching,
Understanding, tolerance, respecting...and,
Forgiving!

The People in the middle of these storms...
Will have the solutions...for,
Saving their families, for...
Future generations!

Blue Bear is full of solutions!

Cause and Effect
Which is positive, and which is
negative? Is there an alternative?

What are we doing, and...
What are we becoming?
We may need to do some investigating!
For that...
We'll go Blue Bearing!

"What do you say, Blue Bear?"
"Cause and effect...
Could be an implement...for,
Cultivating your development...
Becoming self-evident,
Revealing your notable experiment...
Resulting in your achievement!
To avoid, unnecessary difficulties,
You have *cause,* being the object...
With *effect,* offering opportunities,
For you, to collect!
"Thanks Blue Bear!"
Just because we now have electricity,
Doesn't mean candles have no necessity!

Sharing perceptions,
Then on to our confessions!
Supporting the human, with admiration,
Blue Bear assisting us...
With his, administrations!

What our human condition is experiencing...
From movement, to achievement,
Seeing the road ahead...
With less hindrance,

Establishing goals, with a purpose...
Connecting us, to an entrance!

Blue continues:
"You've created a cause...
Now, here comes the effect,
With energy being the key to connect...
Joining together...cause, with all the effects!"

"Thanks Blue!"

Having created a relation-ship,
With kin-ship...
Ready to board our steam-ship...and,
Having installed an inter-com...
Proceeding with love, joy...and,
Wis-dom!

With self-preservation in activation...
Becoming an evaluation:

Using Cause and Effect...to be,
The correct architect!

Experiencing our ability to process knowledge,
Could there be a class for teaching...
Cause and Effect, in college?

With Blue Bear on board,
We could learn from those...
At Mt. Rushmore!
Or!
Having our own college,
With our own, Blue Bear...
Knowledge!
Blue Bear teaching us about the bees...
From gathering the honey,

Yellow Toadster, in his yellow roadster...
Teaching history is not a mystery,
Leon Chameleon exploring time, space, and matter...
Changing from one to another,
Winston Owl, who flies like a kite at night...
Teaching us about geography and flight,
White Rabbit has a light for illumination...
Teaching gardening, cooking, and home renovation,
The Rainbow Toads are ready for classes...
Teaching re-construction, after the storm passes,
Whatever the condition, each colored toad...
Will carry his load,
Lavender, magenta, blue, green, and gold,
Dr. Drake has patients to admit...
With a tummy ache,
Teaching, give and take!

For now, we'll have a pow-wow...
With Blue Bear, enjoying his blue marshmallows,
Yellow Toadster, with his toadstool pillows...
Taking a nap, under the willows,
Where we'll find...
Leon Chameleon, on a branch in the tree,
Sharing his ins and outs of adaptability...
Wise Winston Owl, on a settee,
In a hole in the willow tree...
Waiting for night, and a cool evening breeze,
White Rabbit, on her lounge under the ground...
With the Rainbow Toads, all gathered around,
"Let's do some croaking...
There's no time for loafing!"
Those Toads never stop joking!

Blue Bear College
Where we would learn a lot of knowledge...
Having our own professors,

Covering every subject...
On...*Cause,* with all the *Effects!*

With Blue Bear's imagination and dedication, we can go anywhere, create most anything.

Are our Wishes...Our Intentions?

Wishes are like empty dishes...
Until, we use our intentions!

With the quietness of a Buddha think-king...
I should've, would've, could've,
Prompted an off-spring-ing!

"What are our intentions?
Flying to the moon...or,
Stirring with a spoon?"

Relativity to activity,
Isaac Newton—-to Fig Newton, or...
Blue Bearing for berry sharing!

Our wishes becoming...
Our intentions!

Yes! And always with continuations!

The World is waiting...
For,
The Blue Bear Connection!

After Thoughts

With the Blue Bear, there will always be continuations! "Why?" you say. Very simply. Because every day we are presented with choices, and the Blue Bear energy will be there for our visitations. When consequences come to mind, Blue Bear isn't far behind.

My visitations with Blue Bear will be posted on, "The Blue Bear Energy" website; ready for you to copy, and then, add to your collection, in your own notebook.

Being connected to The Blue Bear Energy is, indeed, a special gift!

Your friend,
Louise

Let Freedom Ring!

From:
Equality...to, Stability...to,
Liberty...to, Singing:
"Let Freedom Ring!"
From:
Building, to...Guarding, to...
Securing, to...Singing:
"Let Freedom Ring!"
From:
Motivation, to...Activation, to...
Liberation, to...Singing:
"Let Freedom Ring!"
"Let Freedom Ring!"
"Let Freedom Ring!"

Yes! We are blessed to be living in a country where we have the freedom to become whatever our heart, mind, and spirit take us.

Printed in the United States
By Bookmasters